SPACE JUNK JOURNEY

Story by Cameron Macintosh

Illustrations by Wan Norazura

Space Junk Journey

Text: Cameron Macintosh
Publishers: Tania Mazzeo and Eliza Webb
Series consultant: Amanda Sutera
Hands on Heads Consulting
Editor: Jarrah Moore
Project editor: Annabel Smith
Designer: Jess Kelly
Project designer: Danielle Maccarone
Illustrations: Wan Norazura
Production controller: Renee Tome

NovaStar

ISBN 978 0 17 033472 3

Cengage Learning Australia
Level 5, 80 Dorcas Street
Southbank VIC 3006 Australia
Phone: 1300 790 853
Email: aust.nelsonprimary@cengage.com

For learning solutions, visit **cengage.com.au**

Printed in China by 1010 Printing International Ltd
1 2 3 4 5 6 7 29 28 27 26 25

Nelson acknowledges the Traditional Owners and Custodians of the lands of all First Nations Peoples. We pay respect to Elders past and present, and extend that respect to all First Nations Peoples today.

Contents

Chapter 1

Crash!

August 2099, Sebton Space Academy. Twins Ruby and Rodrigo are putting their piloting skills into practice.

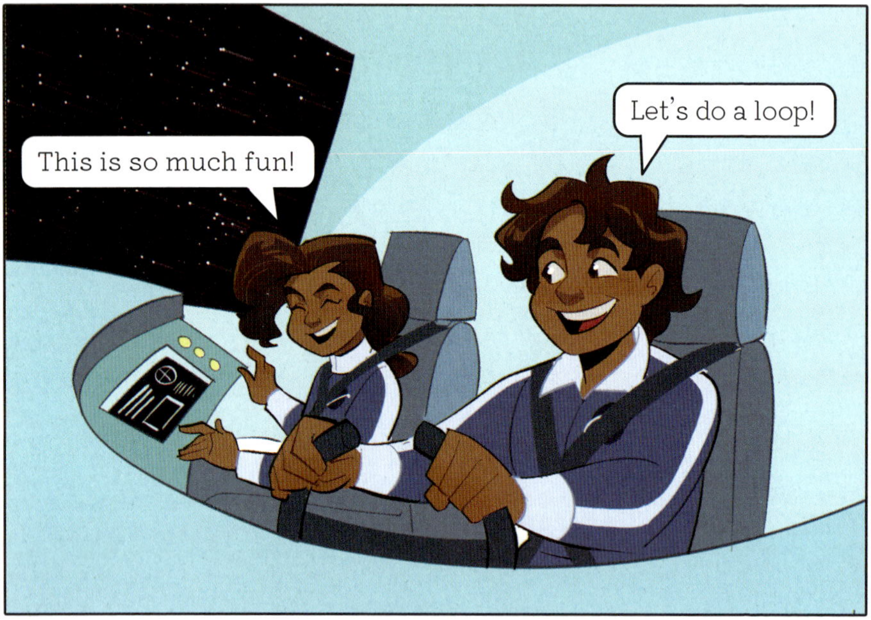

This is so much fun!

Let's do a loop!

But suddenly ...

Watch out, Rodrigo, an old satellite!

Whoa, I'll swerve left!

It's too late! We're going to hit it!

MISSION FAILED

We really blew it this time.

We should have kept a closer eye on the radar.

That was very disappointing. This is a flight simulator, not a video game.

Sorry, Professor Khan. We'll be less acrobatic next time.

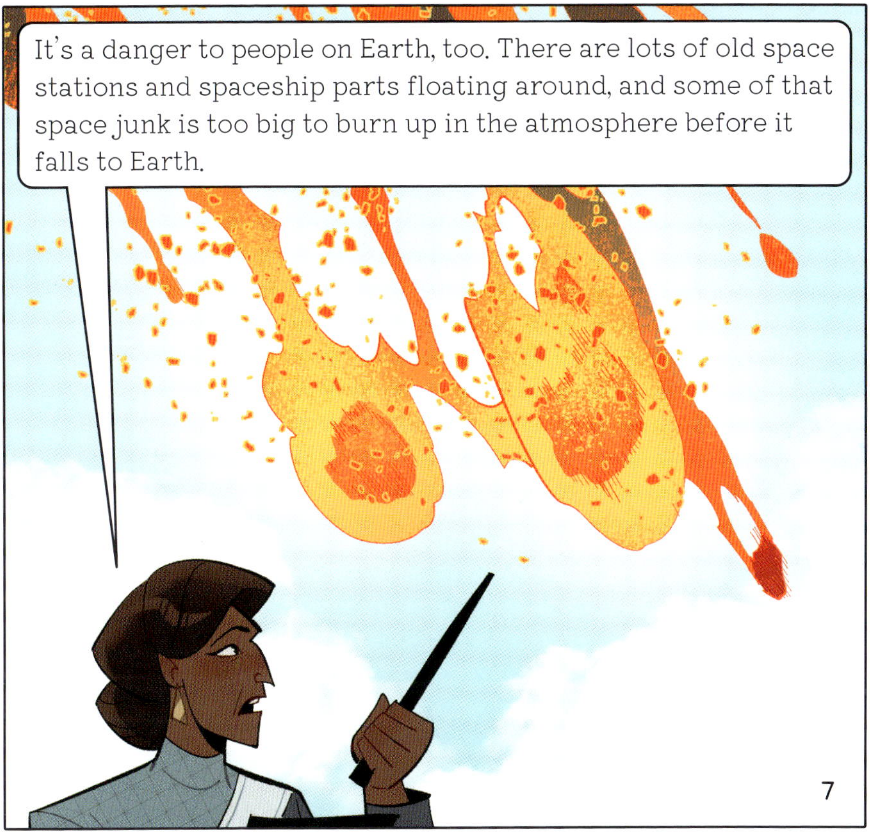

It's a danger to people on Earth, too. There are lots of old space stations and spaceship parts floating around, and some of that space junk is too big to burn up in the atmosphere before it falls to Earth.

Space junk won't crash into us, will it? Earth's a very big pla–
KABOOM
Get down, everyone!

You're right, Ruby, Earth is a big planet.
But there's more than three centuries' worth of space junk up there, and it can land anywhere.

What if a piece of space junk hit the academy, or someone's home?

Exactly. Space junk is a real problem.

Chapter 2

Ruby's Invention

That night, at home ...

I'm going to make a space junk tracker that can warn us when a big piece gets too close to Earth.

What a great idea!

You can do it, Ruby!

Sounds cool. I'd love to help!

Many days and nights pass. Ruby works on her tracker.

Until finally ...

I finished!

Wow, it's **incredible**. It even shows where the space junk will land!

Oh **no**, it looks like the old Argus shuttle is going to re-enter the atmosphere. It's huge – there's no way it'll burn up on its way down!

SPACE JUNK ALERT!

Where will it land?

Greywood Forest ... tomorrow night!

That forest is bone dry. It'll go up in flames!

We need to tell someone!

Let's show Professor Khan tomorrow. She'll know what to do.

The next day, at school ...

This is impressive, Ruby. But according to the Sebton Space Agency, the Argus shuttle is unlikely to crash down for another 500 years.

But, Professor ...

Come on, it's time for class. Don't worry about the Argus.

Later, in the library ...

There must be something wrong with the agency's space junk monitors. It's up to us to save the forest.

The Argus is only **hours** away from re-entering Earth's atmosphere. We need to push it out to a distance of 350 kilometres to put it in a safe orbit.

I have an idea!

Chapter 3

Tangled

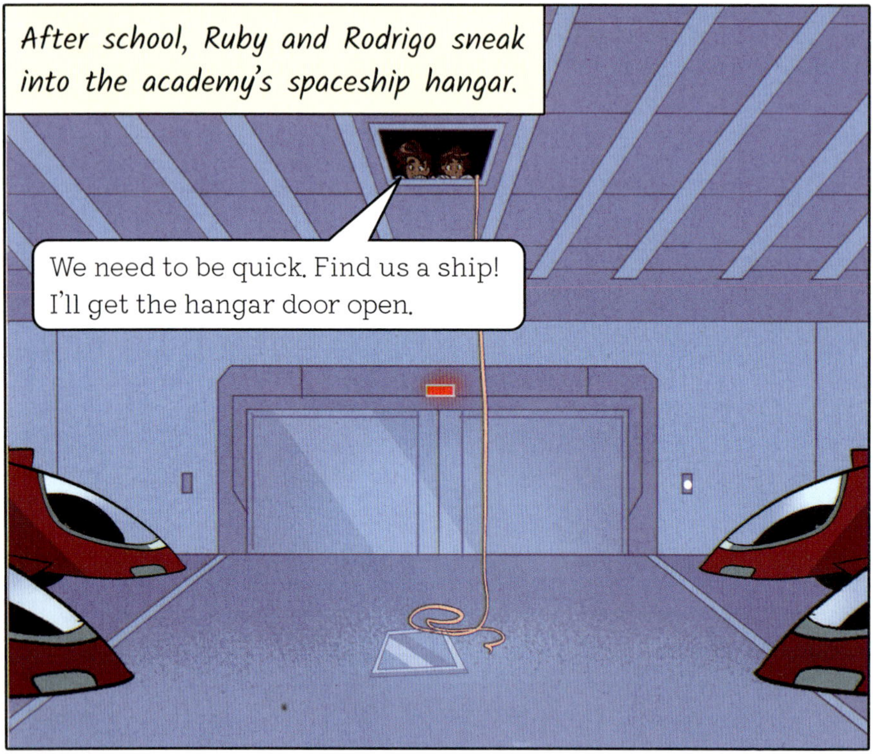

After school, Ruby and Rodrigo sneak into the academy's spaceship hangar.

We need to be quick. Find us a ship! I'll get the hangar door open.

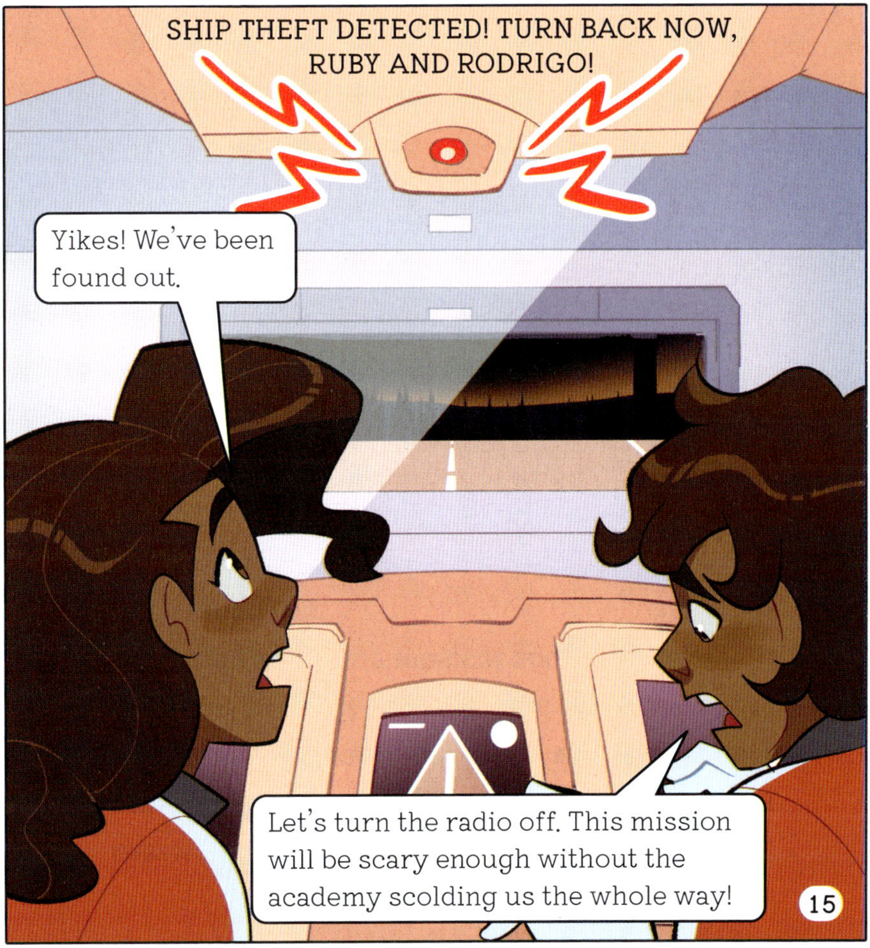

SHIP THEFT DETECTED! TURN BACK NOW, RUBY AND RODRIGO!

Yikes! We've been found out.

Let's turn the radio off. This mission will be scary enough without the academy scolding us the whole way!

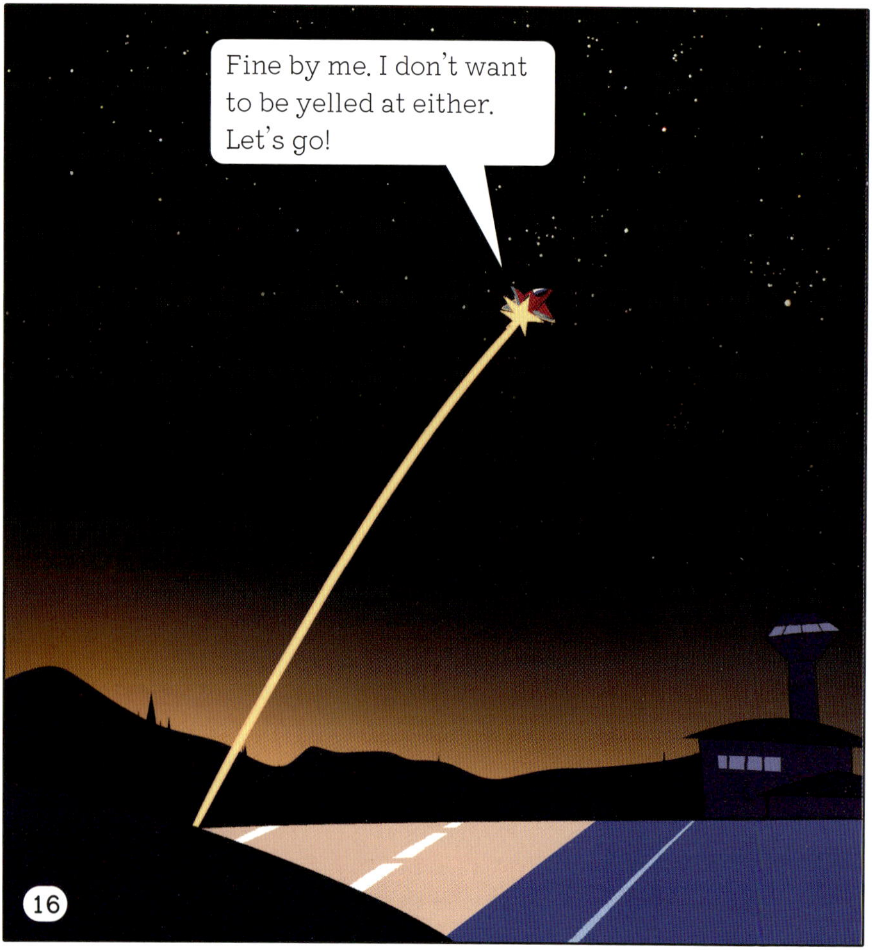

Fine by me. I don't want to be yelled at either. Let's go!

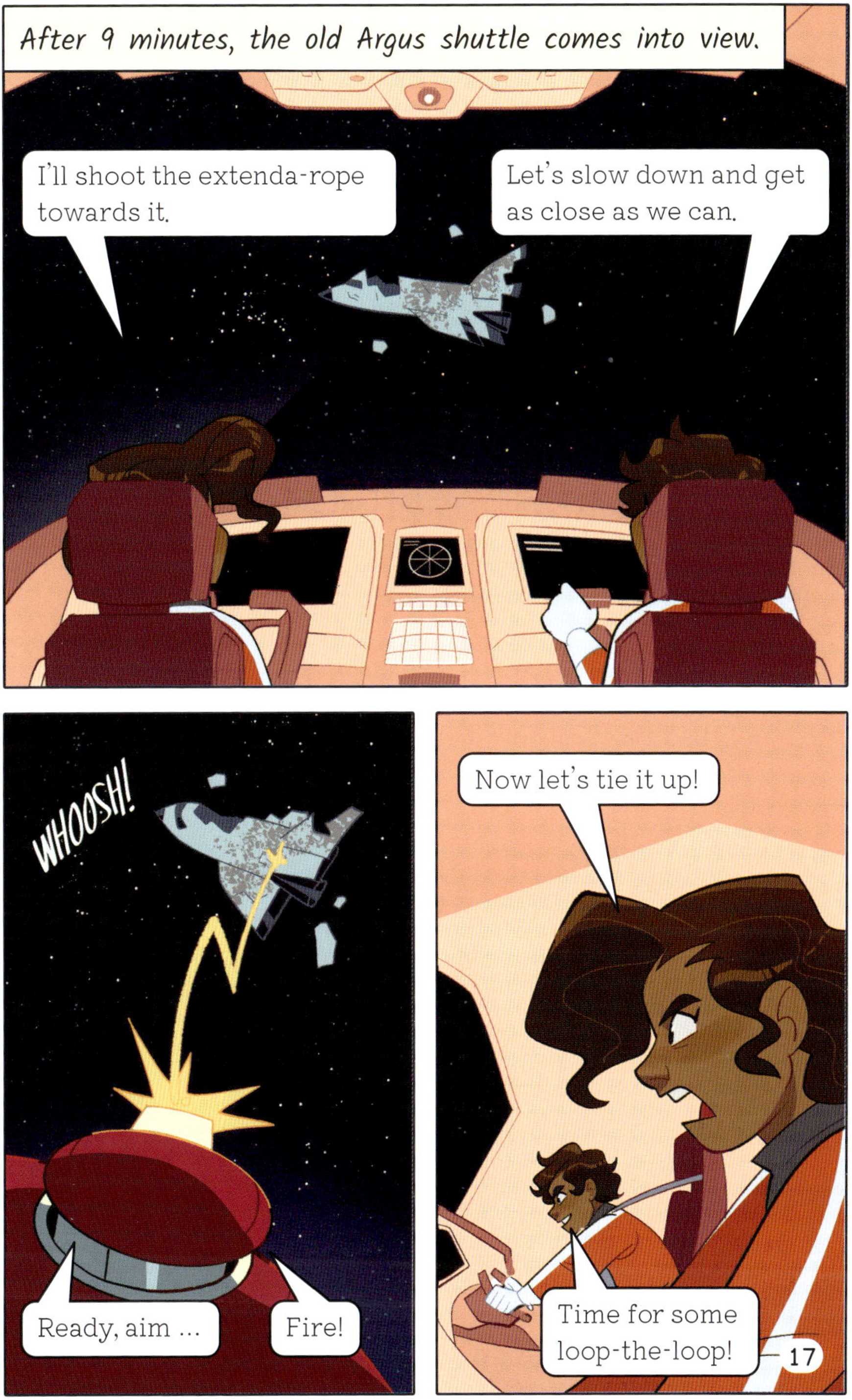

After 9 minutes, the old Argus shuttle comes into view.

I'll shoot the extenda-rope towards it.

Let's slow down and get as close as we can.

Nice piloting, Rodrigo!
Thanks, Ruby! I'll just make sure it's secure. Then we can start dragging it further away from Earth.

Oh no, the left wing's tangled in the rope.

And now we're stuck!

Mayday!
We're stuck to the Argus shuttle, which is going to re-enter Earth's atmosphere in ... 12 minutes!

No reply! I really **did** break the radio.
We're going to have to find a way to cut the extenda-rope ourselves!

Chapter 4

Space Walking

Ruby and Rodrigo pass through the airlock and step out into space.

8 MINUTES
UNTIL RE-ENTRY

It's not working.
The extenda-rope is too strong!

Let's try sawing the rope together at the same spot.

Good thinking. We'll cut in from opposite sides.

6 MINUTES
UNTIL RE-ENTRY

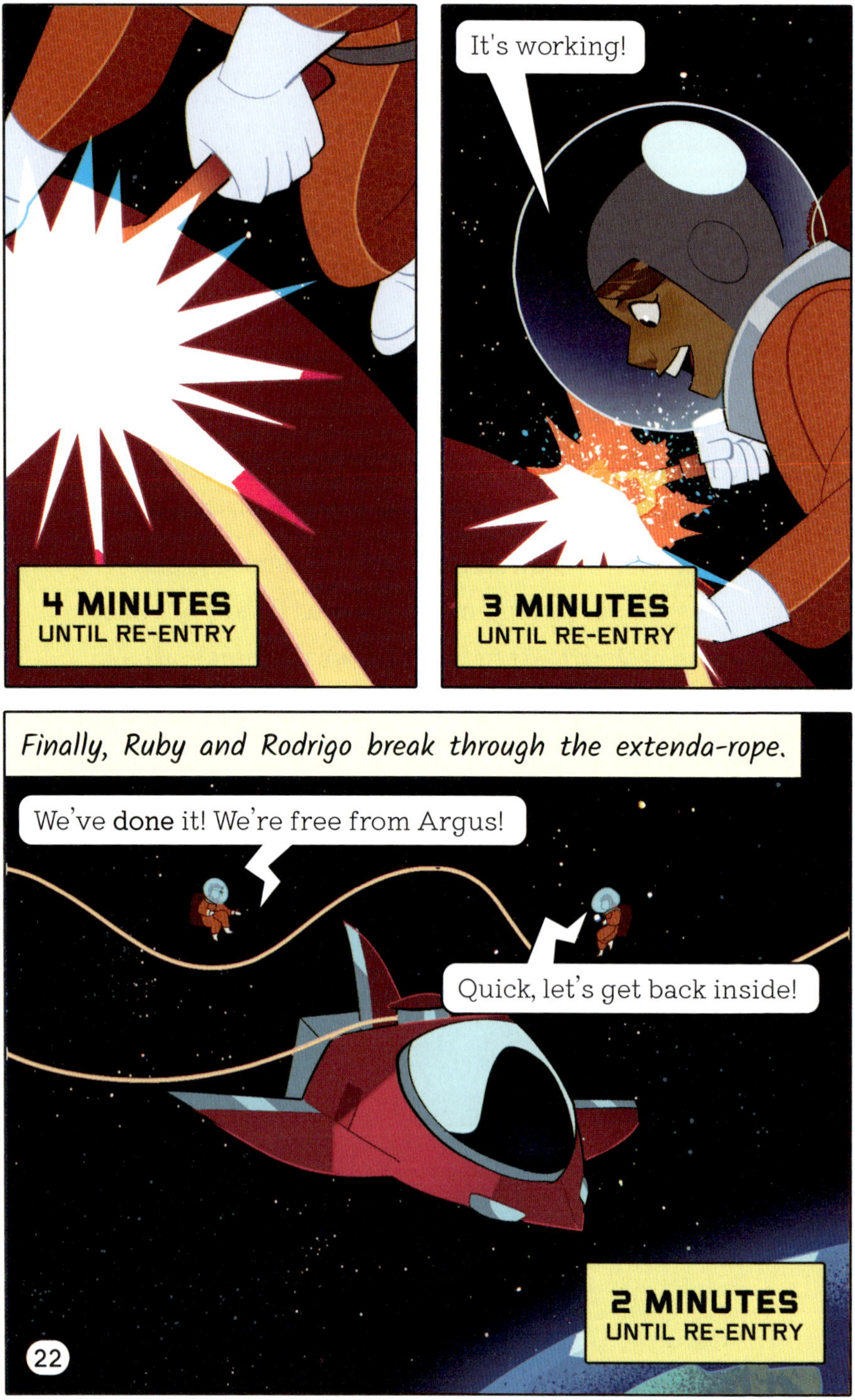

Finally, Ruby and Rodrigo break through the extenda-rope.

We've **done** it! We're free from Argus!

Quick, let's get back inside!

2 MINUTES
UNTIL RE-ENTRY

Back at the controls ...
We've saved ourselves, but in one minute, the Argus is still going to plunge down to Greywood Forest. This has all been for nothing!

Let's fly back to the academy and warn everyone.

This is strange. Why are we moving so slowly?
Is there a problem with the engine?

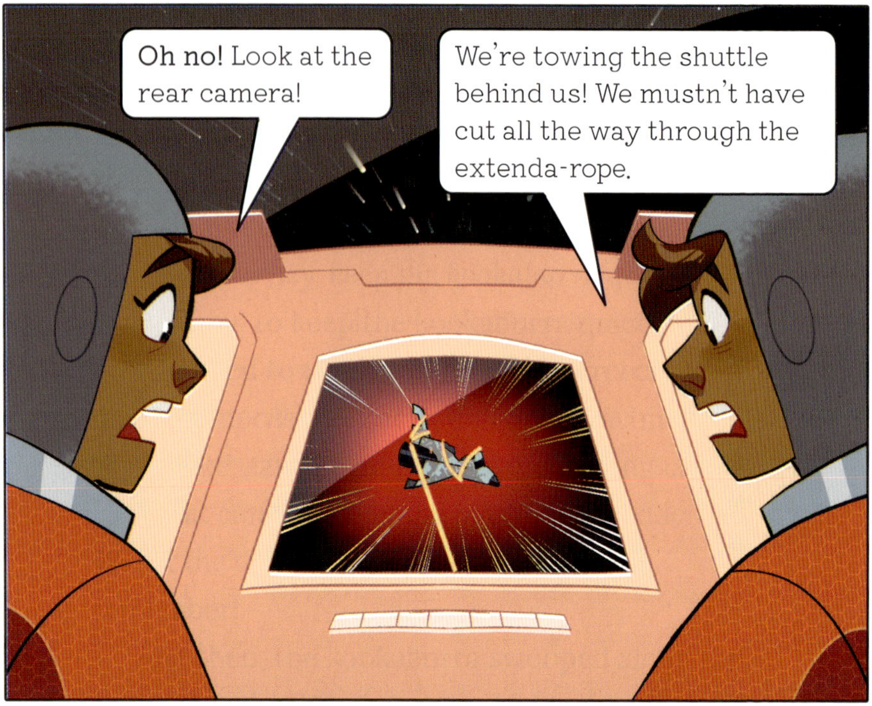

Oh no! Look at the rear camera!

We're towing the shuttle behind us! We mustn't have cut all the way through the extenda-rope.

ZOOM!

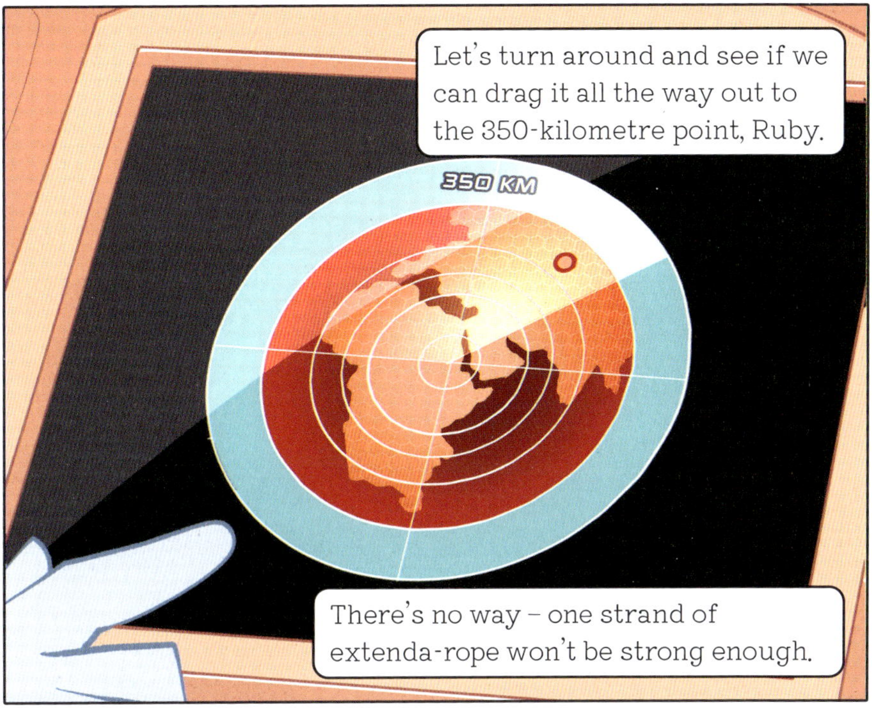

Let's turn around and see if we can drag it all the way out to the 350-kilometre point, Ruby.

350 KM

There's no way – one strand of extenda-rope won't be strong enough.

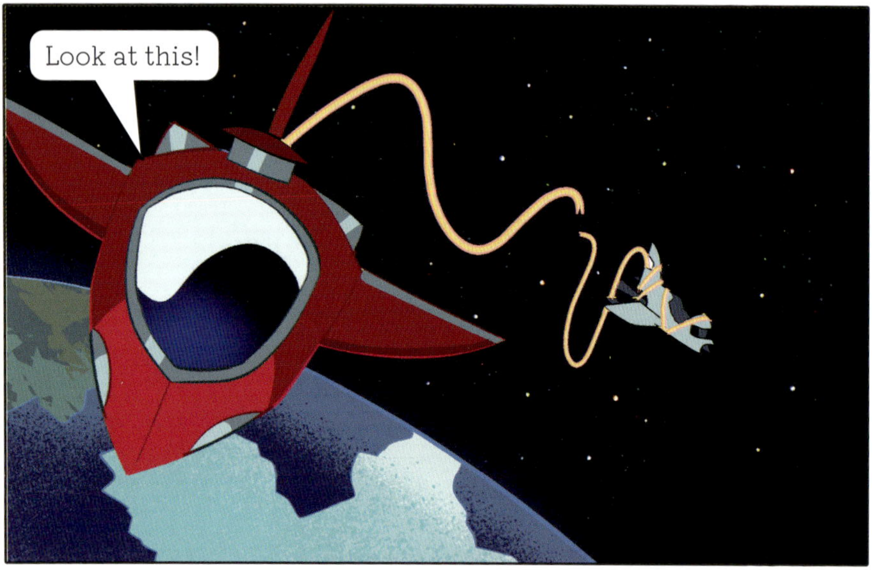

Look at this!

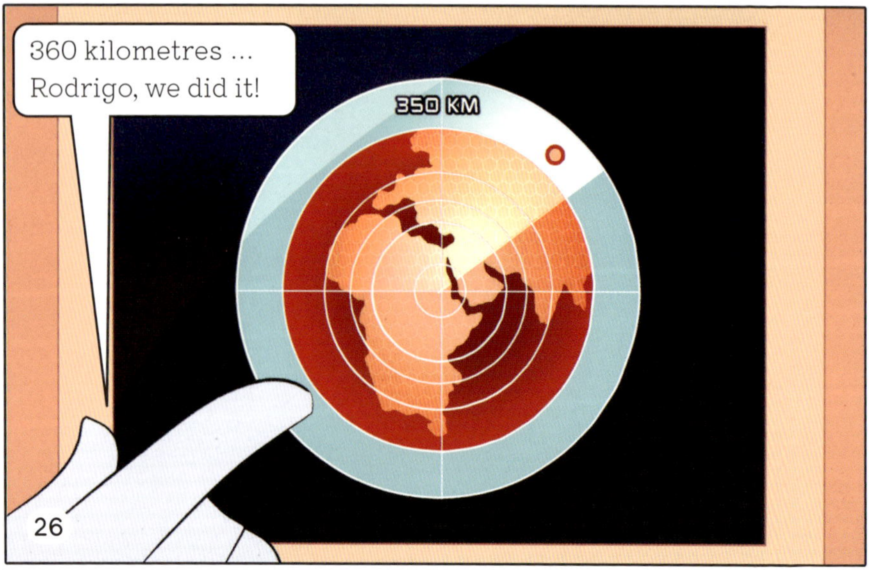

360 kilometres ...
Rodrigo, we did it!

350 KM

Relieved, Ruby and Rodrigo turn their ship back towards Earth.

Let's get back to the academy and see how much trouble we're in …

The forest should be safe, now. Mission accomplished!

Ruby, look! We're on TV!

We really **are** in trouble.

Ruby and Rodrigo safely land the ship back at the Space Academy.
There's Professor Khan.
I can see Mum and Dad, too! And a bunch of reporters!

Your space junk tracker was right all along, Ruby. You saved Greywood Forest! I'm sorry I didn't take your warning more seriously.

Well done, kids.

But please tell us what you're doing the next time you save the planet!

Chapter 5

The Famous Junk Tracker!

Ruby and Rodrigo's successful mission is soon big news around the world.

SPACE ACADEMY STUDENTS' DARING MISSION SAVES **GREYWOOD FOREST!**

The Sebton Space Academy works with Ruby to make more trackers ...

... and the local space agency asks Ruby for its own tracker!

So, what's our next adventure, Ruby?
Let's make a star tracker and take people on tours around the Milky Way!
I'll happily be the pilot ... if we can get a ship with a working radio!
The End